To my parents, Barry and Krista Quiner, who have encouraged me more than they know.

To watch videos of Michelle's performances, please search for her on YouTube
and follow her on Instagram: michellequiner.

Printed in the United States of America
First Edition

Photo Credits:
All photographs were provided by the Quiner family, unless otherwise noted.

ISBN-10:   0-9643460-60
ISBN-13:   978-0964346062

Hi! My name is Michelle Quiner. I am a dancer. I am the second oldest of eight children. I have five sisters (who all dance!) and two brothers. I am home schooled, which is very helpful since I spend so much time at the dance studio.

I began dancing at the age of two at the Art of Dance in Chester, New Jersey. I have loved performing for as long as I can remember. When I was three years old, my first performance took place in our dance classroom for our families. I had a sore throat and did not feel very well, but my mom asked me if I still wanted to go. Much to her surprise, I said, "Yes!" I just couldn't miss it!

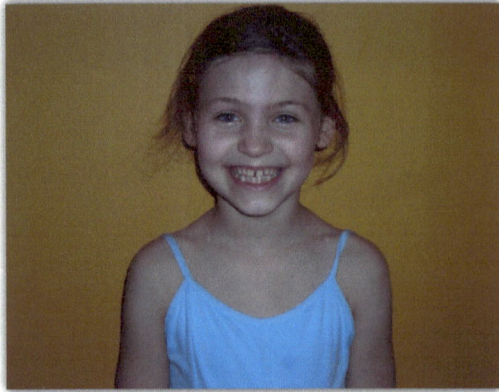

At age six, I was asked to join the Art of Dance Performing Company. My older sister, Jillian, had joined the Company the year before. I was excited to be a part of it, too. My first competition routine was a group tap dance. Since tap is not my best thing, my spot for most of the dance was in the back line. Still, I enjoyed the thrill of being on stage and receiving ribbons for a job well done.

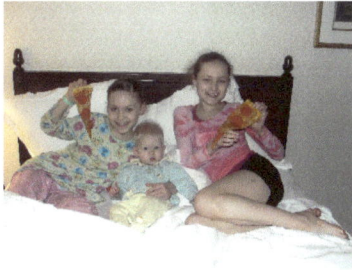

At my studio, in order to perform a solo at a competition you had to win a national scholarship at a regional workshop run by the New York City Dance Alliance (NYCDA). I first tried to earn a scholarship when I was eight years old. The first day of the workshop we learned the audition combination and the second day we performed it for the judges. After watching all 200 of us, they selected around 40 dancers to be finalists. Unfortunately, I did not know the combination at all and was not even selected to be a finalist. One of my friends was chosen, though, so I was very happy for her. My big sister Jillian and I had fun dancing in the workshop classes, staying in a hotel, swimming in the pool, and eating pizza. We also enjoyed competing in our group routines with the other members of the Art of Dance Performing Company. Maybe next year I would practice the combination the night before the audition instead of working on my aerials (but I was so close to getting one!).

At age nine, I was much more motivated to win a national scholarship and earn the chance to perform a solo. I now had attended a few other workshops

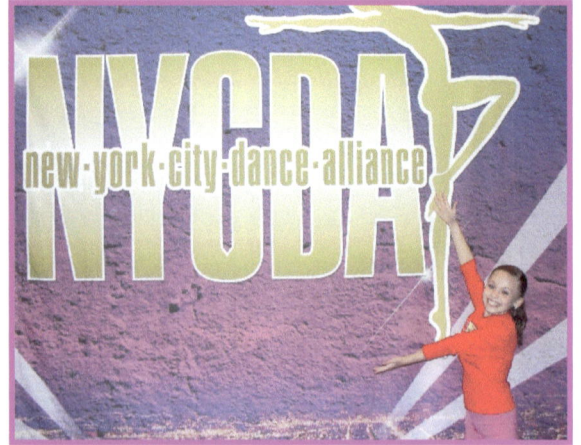

and better understood the audition process, so I was ready when it came time for NYCDA.   The perfect end to a great and inspiring weekend of dance with classes from some of my favorite teachers like Joe Lanteri and Suzi Taylor was hearing my name called as a runner-up national scholarship winner.   I was delighted!   All smiles as I stood on stage proudly holding my scholarship, I eagerly looked forward to attending NYCDA's Outstanding Dancer Program at Nationals and learning my own solo.   My teacher, Linsey O'Neal, chose a beautiful ballet variation from Le Corsaire for me to perform.   I was given a lovely pink tutu covered with sparkles to wear on stage.   When I arrived at NYCDA Nationals, I found waiting for me an Outstanding Dancer jacket with my name sewn onto it.   I was thrilled!

When I was ten years old, I had two big goals for the year: to dance the role of Clara in the Nutcracker and to win a national dance title. At this point, I was taking dance classes six days a week and usually two or more classes each day. I tried to take at least one ballet class a day. I also trained at two different dance schools. The first was my original studio and the second was a school that focused more on ballet, the North Jersey School of Dance Arts in Hackettstown, NJ.

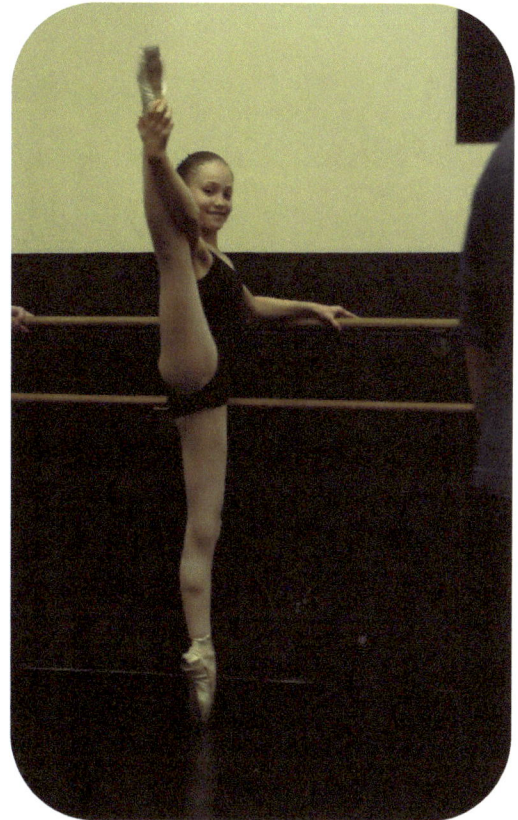

I had performed in my first Nutcracker when I was eight years old and loved the rehearsals from the start. I would be at the studio for four hours and it would feel like four minutes. When the curtains closed after the final show, I was very sad. The magic of once again dancing in the Christmas show felt eons away. Many young ballerinas dream of being Clara one day, and I was no exception. My third year dancing in the Nutcracker, I hoped my time had come. Still, when the cast list went up with my name as Clara … I couldn't believe it! I was going to perform the starring role in the New Jersey Civic Youth Ballet's Nutcracker! On stage, every moment felt like a wonderful dream. I must confess that as I lay in bed the night after the last show, I cried, knowing my time in the spotlight was over.

After an exciting week at NYCDA Nationals, I entered Onstage New York (ONY) Nationals as well. In order to win the title, I needed to come out with the highest score after being evaluated in a jazz class, a tap class, a ballet class, an interview on stage, and my solo. Unfortunately, on the day I had to perform my solo, I woke up with a stomach virus. I remember lying on the floor feeling weak and wondering how I could ever dance my solo. Somehow I managed to get through it. My mom said I did a really good job; maybe it helped that I wasn't as nervous as I might have been. I was very happy to be named one of the top three contestants. That meant I would get to perform my solo a second time, in the Closing Night Gala. I was both nervous and excited. On my final section of pirouettes, the audience gave enthusiastic applause. When Joe Lanteri, the executive director of ONY, announced, "Our new National Miss Mini Onstage is Michelle Quiner from the Art of Dance in Chester, NJ!" my face burst into a huge grin.

While I was in New York City for NYCDA and ONY Nationals, I auditioned for the role of Clara in the Nutcracker portion of the Radio City Christmas Spectacular. The day after the audition, my mom received a call from Radio City offering me the part in the Nashville, TN production. I could not believe it! Dancing in the Radio City Christmas Spectacular was an amazing experience. I loved performing each night at the legendary Grand Ole Opry House. My parents thought I would tire of dancing in so many shows, but I never did. I enjoyed watching the Rockettes and Ensemble Dancers perform as well. They are so talented! Performing as Clara in the Radio City Christmas Spectacular was a dream come true.

After Radio City, I was asked to model dancewear for Costume Gallery and A Wish Come True. It was so much fun to have a stylist do my hair in different ways and to have make-up professionally applied. The costumes were beautiful. The pizza for lunch was great, too! When the catalogs came out later in the year, I couldn't believe my pictures were in them.

When I was eleven, I decided to focus more on ballet, so I began taking classes only at the North Jersey School of Dance Arts. Since this school emphasized performances and ballet competitions, I would have to attend workshops and regular competitions on my own. I liked being able to choose which competitions and workshops to attend, but I missed seeing my friends from the Art of Dance. When I would compete my solo, my family members were usually the only ones cheering for me in the audience. In order to give me a new solo, my mom talked to Suzi Taylor, an amazing teacher from Steps on Broadway and NYCDA, during a workshop. Suzi agreed to choreograph a contemporary dance solo for me called "Pretty Good Year". I loved it. It fit me perfectly!

Dance workshops are so much fun! Jillian and I usually travel to several each year, including NYCDA, Jump, Nuvo Dance Convention, Adrenaline, Artists Simply Human (ASH), 24 Seven Dance Convention, and West Coast Dance Explosion (WCDE). I really enjoy learning new combinations from top choreographers and seeing my friends from other dance studios. Most workshops hold an audition for scholarships to future dance events. I like to wear bright colors such as hot pink or turquoise blue so I can stand out. It's fun to be picked. My mom is also happy when I win a scholarship because workshops are very expensive, especially when you have a big family!

Every dancer has a story or two about a negative audition experience. I remember attending Nuvo Dance Convention when I was eleven years old. At this point, I had been going to workshops for several years and been awarded many scholarships. I prefer to stand in the front line during auditions so I can be seen. At the Nuvo audition I got a great spot right in the center of the front line. The judges watched as I began dancing the combo. I started strongly … but all of a sudden my mind went blank and I forgot what came next! Unfortunately there were no demonstrators doing the combo in front of us. I was so embarrassed! Sadly, I was not even chosen to be a finalist and I did not receive a scholarship. I was very upset with myself and it was hard to finish classes that day. The incident unnerved me a bit, and I found it difficult in future auditions not to worry about making the same mistake. I began hiding in the back and failing to win the scholarships I was usually awarded. My mom talked to me about my fear and told me that I needed to push myself and not be afraid. She told me that standing in the front and remembering the combination makes me a winner, even if I don't receive a scholarship. With her words in mind, I started challenging myself again in auditions and nursed my confidence back to health.

14

One of my favorite competitions is Starpower. I attended one of the competition's regional events and my "Pretty Good Year" solo won first place! I received a free title entry for Starpower Nationals. I really wanted to compete at Nationals, and Starpower was holding one of its national events in late June in Uncasville, CT, only 3 hours away from my home. There was one problem, however: my mom was due with a baby on June 20! Thankfully, my grandpa agreed to take me to CT. As it turned out, my little brother was born a week late, the day before I had to leave for the competition. On June 28, Grandpa and I set out for the Constitution State … but not without first stopping by the hospital to see David's cute little face! I had a blast at the competition and was overjoyed to receive first place and the title of Miss Junior Starpower. My grandpa could barely fit the trophies in his car; they were taller than he was!

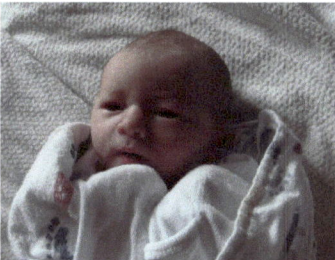

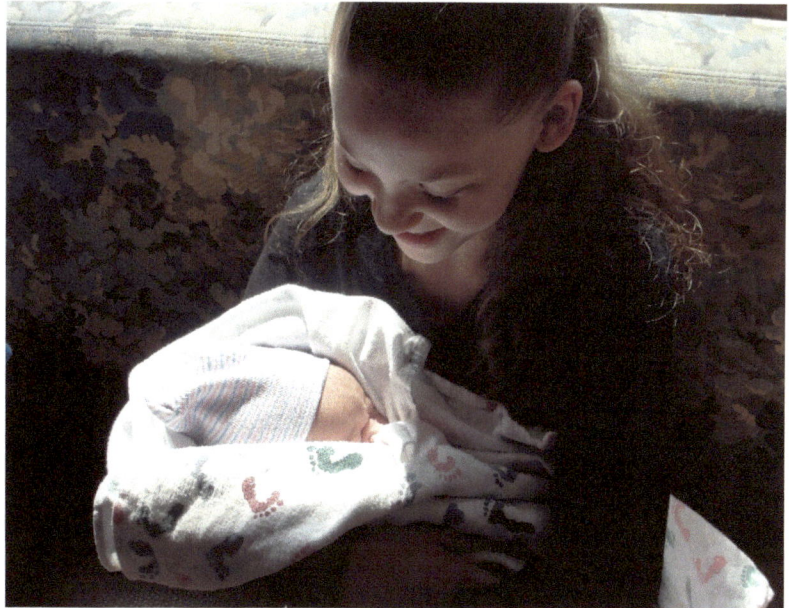

At Starpower Nationals there was a television crew filming for an upcoming reality show called "Dance Moms". The show had not yet begun airing so we did not know what it would be about. I ended up competing against Chloe Lukasiak. She came in fourth place and did not seem too happy. I had to sign waivers in case they used footage from my solo on the show. I didn't make it on the show, but it's cool to know that Abby Lee Miller watched me perform in the gala. Sometime later I was asked to do a Skype interview for her new television show, "Abby Lee's Ultimate Dance Competition". They asked for a picture of me surrounded by my trophies. I was not asked to join the show, but that was okay with me. I am a shy person, so it might not have been a right fit for me.

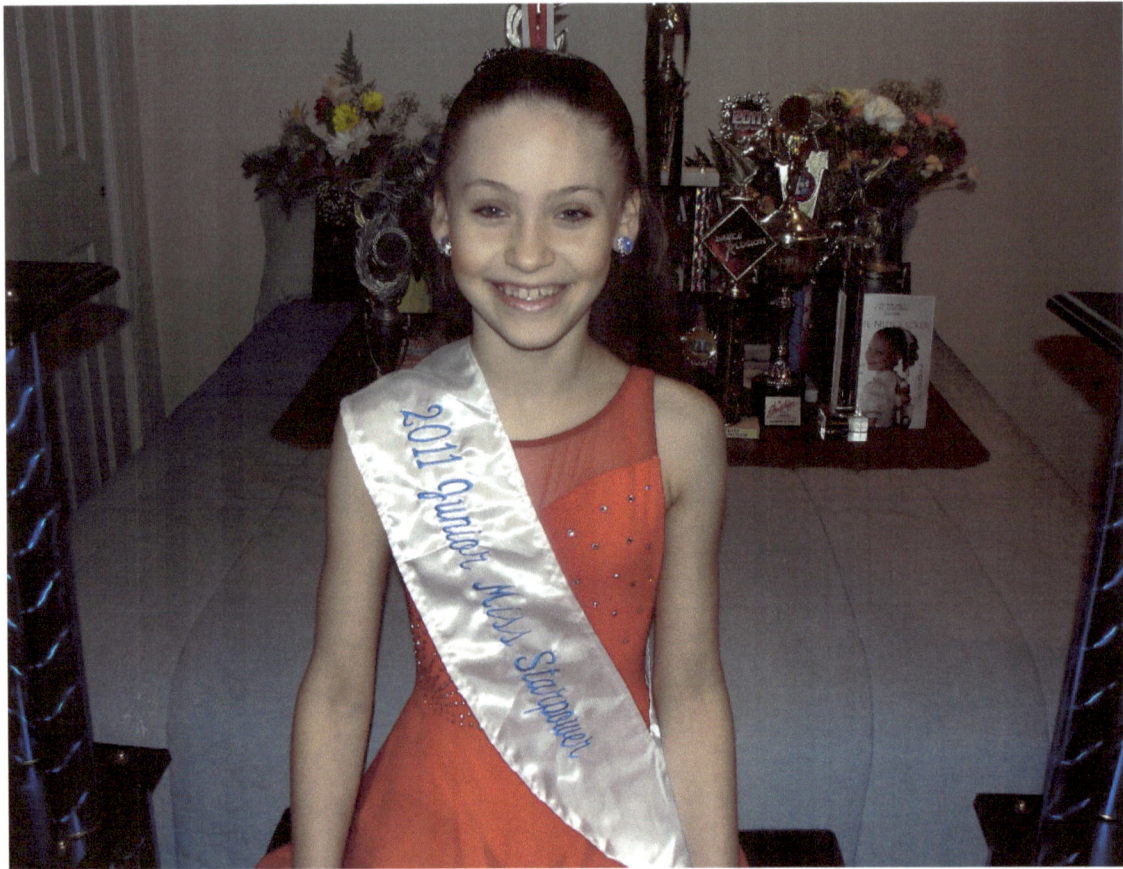

In addition to regular dance competitions, I also really enjoy attending ballet competitions. My favorite one is Youth America Grand Prix (YAGP). The movie *First Position* follows a few dancers' journeys through YAGP's competition process. I have watched it so many times! The competition is very challenging and only the top few dancers in each category make it to Nationals. You have to score a 95 or higher to qualify. I entered the Torrington, CT regional. I performed a contemporary solo and a ballet variation from Don Quixote. I was surprised and honored to win the first place award. The judges had dubbed me the top female in the Pre-Competitive category! I was thrilled to score highly enough to advance to Nationals with some of the best ballet dancers from around the world.

Later I again auditioned for Clara in the Radio City Christmas Spectacular. Due to problems with the economy, the number of locations for the show had been reduced. This meant that instead of the usual twelve Claras, only six girls would be hired for the role. Despite this, I thought I had a good chance of getting the part. I was still under the 4'10" height limit. The audition went well and my hopes were high. Every time the phone rang, I would ask my mom if it was Radio City calling to offer me the part. When the deadline passed and I realized I had not been picked, I was heartbroken. I cried. My parents hugged me. They felt so bad for me. I was very disappointed. I had really wanted to dance in the show again, having loved being a part of the renowned Christmas production and performing night after night for thousands of people.

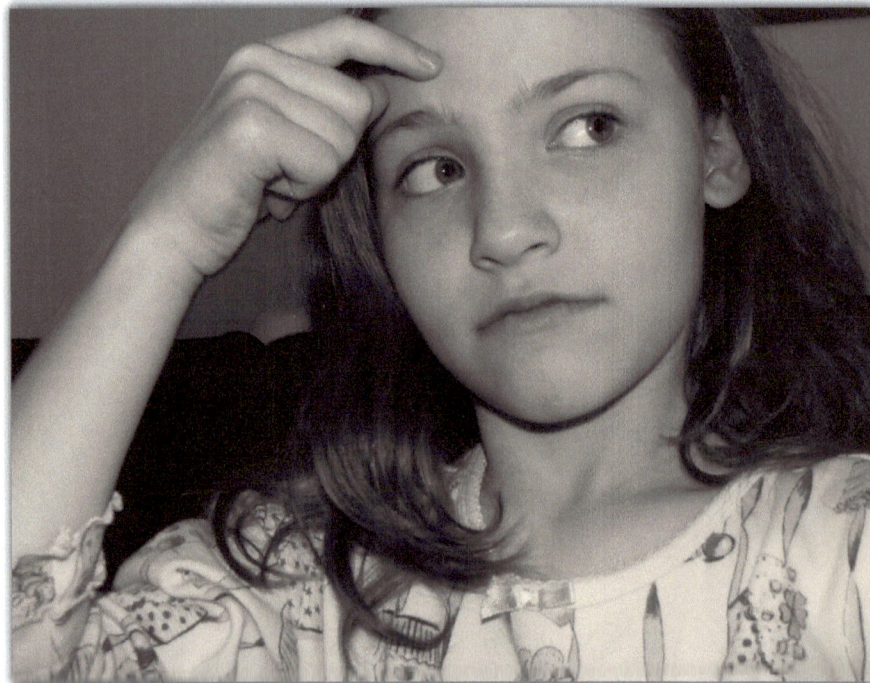

When I was twelve, my parents surprised me with another solo from Suzi Taylor.   Suzi is one of my favorite workshop teachers so of course I was thrilled.   This new routine called "The Rain" really showed off my flexibility.   I loved competing my solo.   I would have performed it every weekend had my parents let me.   Regardless of whether I'm competing or just performing, being on stage always fills my heart with joy.

"The Rain" was received very well at the regional competitions.   The judges at Adrenaline gave my solo the highest score of all the dances, including the group routines.   One judge, Justin Giles, gave me a perfect score!

For several years now two of my goals had been to place at NYCDA Nationals and at The Dance Awards (then the national finals for Jump and Nuvo Dance Convention), but so far I had always come up short. This year would be my last as a Junior before advancing to the Teen category, which seemed like a huge jump.   At both

competitions I felt good about my dancing during my solo performance and the accompanying auditions.   When Joe Lanteri of NYCDA announced my name in the Top Twelve, I was so excited!   It was a moment I will never forget.   I also made the Top Ten at The Dance Awards and got to participate in a special improv audition in front of many cheering people. It was scary … but definitely fun as well!

When I was thirteen years old, I hoped to get a new solo for the upcoming competition season.   My dad lost his job, however, which meant we would need to reduce some of our dance expenses.   My mom gave me the choice between creating my own solo and repeating the same one from last year.   While I really liked "The Rain", I decided to try

choreographing my own routine because I wanted something new. Thankfully, I found a great piece of music from Brian Crain, ironically called "Rain".   With my dad's help I cut the music to meet the time requirements at the different competitions. I titled my contemporary dance "Alone".   In the evening, when dance classes were over, I would piece together my solo in our family room. The process took several weeks.   I wondered how the finished product would fare in competition.   Would my solo look professional enough?

At one of Turn It Up Dance Challenge's regional events, I was shocked to hear my solo named the highest scoring routine for the entire competition. My mom entered the video from that competition into two online contests held by Harlequin Floors and Dance Media, respectively. Harlequin Floors awarded me $250 and Dance Media gave me a scholarship to Joffrey Ballet's summer program in New York. I also entered one of Starpower's regional events where I again won first place and received a free title entry for Nationals. One month later I traveled to Uncasville, CT to compete with over 200 other Teens vying for the top spot. I was stunned to hear my name called as the first place winner and recipient of a $500 prize. A few weeks later I attended Legacy Dance Championships's national finals at the Jersey Shore, where I also received first place. I was later awarded the national title of Miss Teen Onstage New York. This turned out to be my best year yet!

Next year I plan again to choreograph my own solo, as well as my younger sister's. I have learned so much through competing and performing dance. I am grateful to my family, my dance teachers, and the competition judges for their encouragement, support, and advice. I love to dance and dream of someday becoming a professional dancer.

About the Author

Michelle Quiner was featured in the July/August 2014 issue of *Dance Spirit* magazine as the *You Should Know* dancer.   She has won several national titles including Miss Mini Onstage New York, Miss Junior Starpower, Miss Teen Onstage New York, and Miss Starpower.   She has participated in the YAGP finals in New York, danced in the final round at the World Ballet Competition, and been named a bronze medalist at the Valentina Kozlova International Ballet Competition.   She has also placed in the Top Eight at NYCDA Nationals and the Top Ten at The Dance Awards.

Michelle has performed as Clara for the Radio City Christmas Spectacular and the Sugar Plum Fairy for the New Jersey Civic Youth Ballet.   She has earned summer intensive scholarships to the Pittsburgh Ballet Theatre, Joffrey Ballet New York, and the Valentina Kozlova Dance Conservatory.   She has also received various scholarships at dance workshops such as New York City Dance Alliance, Jump, Nuvo Dance Convention, 24 Seven Dance Convention, West Coast Dance Explosion, Artists Simply Human, and Adrenaline.   Michelle's solos have been awarded first place overall at regional competitions such as Believe, Beyond the Stars, Dance Xplosion, Kids Artistic Revue, Hall of Fame Dance Challenge, Imagine Dance Challenge, Legacy Dance Championships, National Dance Showcase, On Stage America, Onstage New York, Sheer Talent Ltd., Starstruck, Star Systems, Starpower, StarQuest, Turn It Up Dance Challenge, VIP Dance, and World-Class Talent Experience. She is the recipient of the Sarah Gooch Bradford Memorial Scholarship and the Harlequin Floors Judges' Choice Scholarship.   Michelle models dancewear for Discount Dance Supply, Costume Gallery, and A Wish Come True.

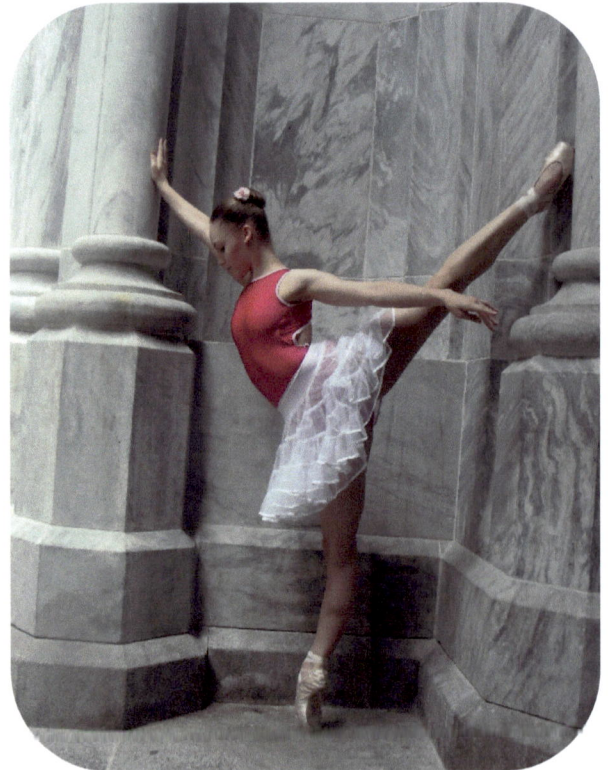

www.ingramcontent.com/pod-product-compliance
Lightning Source LLC
Chambersburg PA
CBHW041223040426
42443CB00002B/75